DISCARDED

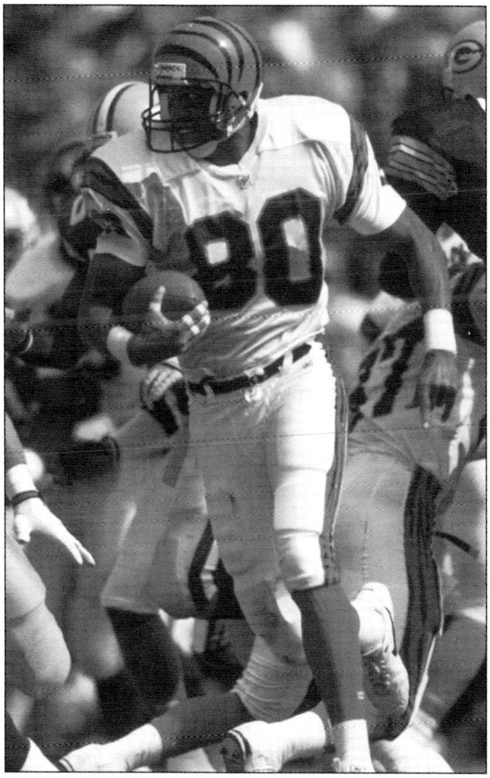
80

NFL★TODAY

CINCINNATI
BENGALS

LOREN STANLEY

CREATIVE EDUCATION

Published by Creative Education
123 South Broad Street, Mankato, Minnesota 56001
Creative Education is an imprint of The Creative Company

Designed by Rita Marshall
Cover illustration by Rob Day

Photos by: Allsport Photography, Associated Press, Bettmann Archive, Duomo, Focus on Sports, Fotosport, and SportsChrome.

Copyright © 1997 Creative Education.
International copyrights reserved in all countries.
No part of this book may be reproduced in any form without written permission from the publisher.
Printed in the United States of America.

Library of Congress Cataloging-in-Publication Data

Stanley, Loren, 1951-
Cincinnati Bengals / by Loren Stanley.
p. cm. — (NFL Today)
Summary: Traces the history of the team from its beginnings through 1996.
ISBN 0-88682-812-0

1. Cincinnati Bengals (Football team)—History—Juvenile literature.
[1. Cincinnati Bengals (Football team) 2. Football—History.]
I. Title. II. Series.

GV956.C54S83   1996   96-15233
796.332'64'0977178—dc20

123456

Cincinnati is known as the "Queen City." Located in the southwest corner of Ohio, Cincinnati is the third largest city in the state. It is also a major port along the majestic Ohio River, which flows west into the Mississippi.

Cincinnati may be called the Queen City, but it was named after a general—Cincinnatus, a famed leader in ancient Rome during the fifth century B.C. The ancient Romans were known for their love of athletics. Likewise Cincinnati, which was home to the first professional baseball team in the United States, the Cincinnati Reds. The city has always had a love for sports and, since 1968, a love for its pro football team, the Cincinnati Bengals.

All-time Cincinnati great Lemar Parrish (#20).

1972

Quarterback Ken Anderson passed for over 1,900 yards during the season.

In the late 1960s, the old American Football League decided to put a team in Cincinnati. But who would run the team? The answer was simple: the same man who built the other pro football team in the state of Ohio. Paul Brown is the only man to have had a professional football team named after him. Brown was the architect of the Cleveland Browns, one of the most successful teams in the history of the National Football League. In 1962, Brown retired. But when he heard the Bengals were being formed, he jumped at the chance to lead them. Brown became more than a leader for the Bengals. He was owner, general manager, and coach.

The Bengals weren't winners at first, but it didn't take Brown long to make them a successful team. In only their third year of play, Cincinnati won the Central Division of the American Football Conference. (The NFL and AFL merged in 1970.) The team was loaded with young stars such as running back Essex Johnson, middle linebacker Bill Bergey, defensive tackle Mike Reid, and cornerback Lemar Parrish. The foundation for a championship team was in place, and Brown knew that he needed a great quarterback.

BROWN FINDS A QUARTERBACK

His choice for the job was Ken Anderson. Most NFL teams didn't know about Anderson when he was drafted in 1971. The reason was that Anderson had played for tiny Augustana College. What would happen to him in jam-packed stadiums in the NFL? "As it turned out," Paul Brown remarked, "it never bothered him a bit because he had been born with poise, and from the start, he looked like a veteran."

A Paul Brown favorite, running back James Brooks (page 7).

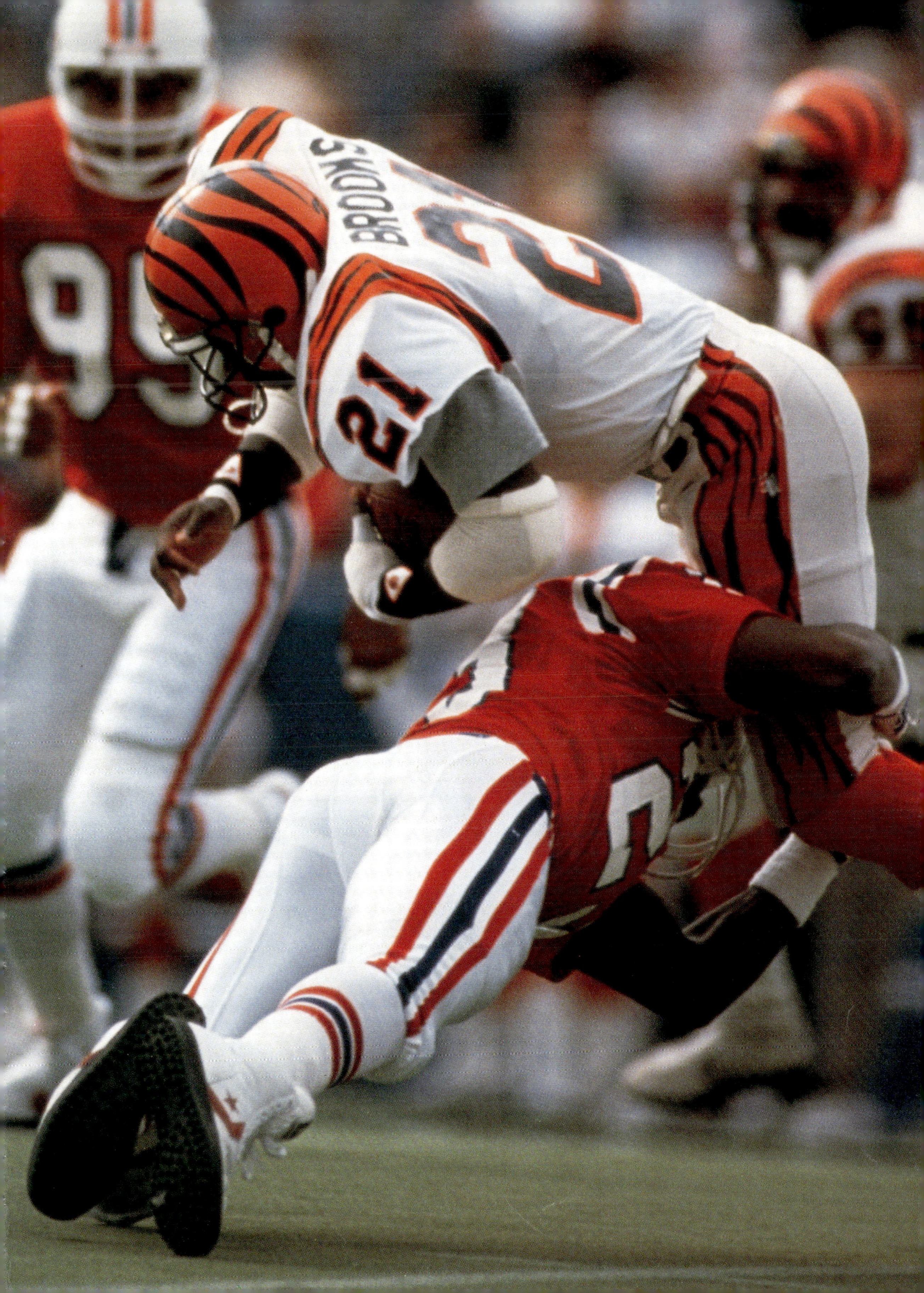
BROOKS
21

1 9 6 7

Paul Brown named his new team the Bengals after former Cincinnati teams of the 1930s and '40s.

By his second year, Anderson was the Bengals' first-string quarterback. In his book, *The Paul Brown Story*, the Bengals coach compared Anderson with Otto Graham, who had led Brown's Cleveland team to several championships.

"Ken ranks just behind Otto Graham as my best quarterback ever. He has all of Otto's physical talents, as well as that one tremendously important attribute for any topflight quarterback—stability."

Led by the skilled quarterback, the Bengals won the Central Division title in 1973 and made the playoffs again in 1975. Anderson became known as one of the most accurate passers in pro football. In one game in 1974 against the Pittsburgh Steelers, Anderson completed 20 out of 22 passes.

During that 1974 season, Cincinnati tight end Bob Trumpy played the entire year with an injured left elbow. "I couldn't button my shirt, and I couldn't brush my teeth," Trumpy said. "Ken knew about it, and he'd throw to where I could bend my arm and catch it. That's how accurate he was. It was like he was saying, 'I know you can't catch with your left hand, so I'll take care of it.' And he did. I probably owe him that one year of my career."

During the mid-1970s, the Bengals were consistent contenders in the AFC Central Division. Anderson had plenty of help on offense from dangerously fast wide receiver Isaac Curtis and elephant-like running back Charles "Boobie" Clark.

WILLIAMS LEADS BY EXAMPLE

Despite this talent, the Bengals started to fade at the end of the 1970s. They became one of the worst teams in pro football. Anderson played well, but something was lacking. The

Bengals needed a defensive leader, one like Anderson was for the offense. By 1981 the team had found that leader, a man who was as forceful off the field as he was on the field. His name was Reggie Williams.

While growing up, Williams wasn't even interested in sports. He wanted to be an outstanding student, but he had a problem. Reggie Williams was born partially deaf. His teachers thought he was a slow learner, and Williams was put in a class with children who had learning problems. But Reggie did not have a learning problem. He had a *hearing* problem. Williams soon was back in regular classes, and several teachers helped him overcome his hearing impairment. Williams never forgot their kindness, and he worked hard to become a good student.

By the time he reached high school, WIlliams was also a sports fan. "As a child, I had very few heroes who let me down," Williams remembered. "Willie Lanier of Kansas City was one of my idols. He was the first black middle linebacker, 'the quarterback of the defense.'" Williams wanted to be like Lanier, but, he said, "I wasn't that good."

Williams went to college at Dartmouth, one of the best schools in the country. At Dartmouth, Williams developed into a very good football player, so good that the Bengals drafted him in 1975. Williams wound up playing for the Bengals for 15 years as an outside linebacker.

As talented as Williams was on the field, he was even more important to the city of Cincinnati when he wasn't playing football. He gave much of his free time to charity. One of those charities was the Cincinnati Speech and Hearing Center for Children. Williams remembered how teachers had helped him with his hearing problems, which also affected his speech. The center was always in need of money, and Williams somehow

Wide receiver Isaac Curtis caught forty-five passes in his rookie season.

Running back Harold Green sparked the offense in the 1990s (pages 10-11).

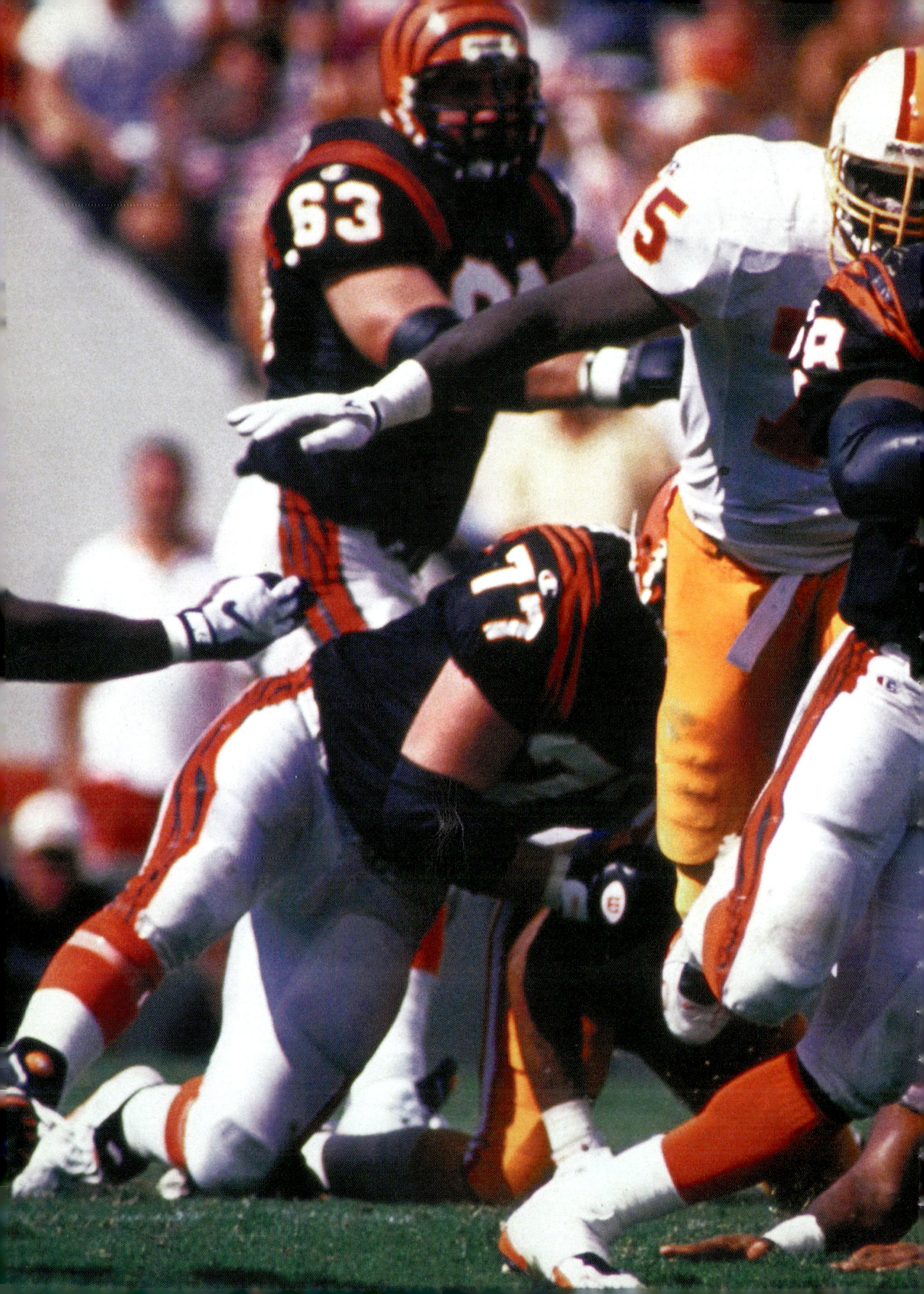
63
77

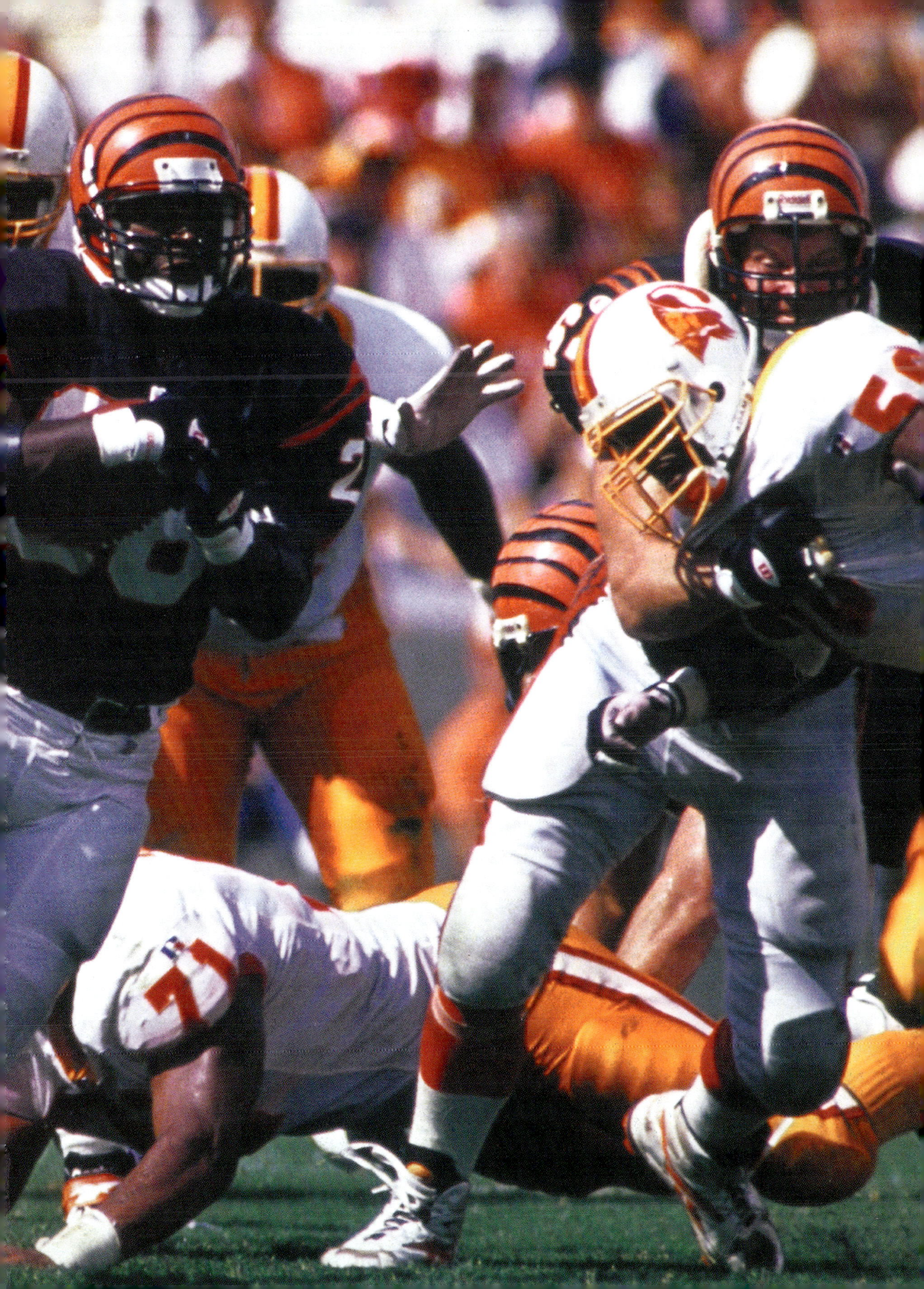

1 9 8 1

Bruising Bengals fullback Pete Johnson rushed for 1,077 yards, averaging 3.9 yards per carry.

managed to raise it. "He finds ways," said Dr. Carol Leslie, director of the center. "He's such an excellent public speaker, and usually he talks about his own experience with hearing impairment."

"There's always time to demonstrate to other people that you care," Williams said. "And one moment of caring can set in motion a whole series of events that can have a positive impact on somebody's life."

Williams was also having a positive impact on the field. He and fellow linebacker Jim LeClair keyed a defense that became very stingy in 1981. Defensive linemen Ross Browner and Eddie Edwards made life miserable for opposing quarterbacks. So did defensive backs Ken Riley and Louis Breeden.

What really made the Bengals successful in 1981, though, was the offense. Ken Anderson was named AFC Player of the Year. He set team records for most yards passing (3,754 yards) and most touchdown passes (29) in a season. In addition, Pete Johnson broke the team single season rushing record with 1,077 yards and also scored 16 touchdowns, another Bengals record.

Led by the offense, Cincinnati went 12-4 and won the AFC Central Division. Playoff victories over Buffalo and San Diego put the Bengals in the Super Bowl for the first time. In that game, Cincinnati fell behind San Francisco 20-0 at halftime, but Anderson rallied the team in the second half. With wide receivers Isaac Curtis and Cris Collinsworth well covered, Anderson used tight end Dan Ross to perfection. Ross caught a Super Bowl record 11 passes as the Bengals scored 21 second-half points. But San Francisco held on to win 26-21. Cincinnati coach Forrest Gregg, who was only in his second year as Bengals head man, praised his team. "You guys played one heckuva second half," Gregg told the Bengals. "Everybody in Cincinnati is proud of you, and you should take pride in yourselves."

Anderson faced reporters after the game and told them the Bengals would be back. "Getting to the Super Bowl is nice, but winning the Super Bowl is what it's all about. I expect to be there when it happens for this team."

Anderson and Williams continued to be stars for Cincinnati. Anderson led the Bengals to the playoffs in 1982, and Williams had his best year ever in 1983. Reggie had 7.5 quarterback sacks that year, a high number for a linebacker who didn't blitz that much. Williams also recovered four fumbles. Despite the heroics, though, the Bengals finished with a 7-9 record. After the season, Forrest Gregg left to take the head

Wide receiver Eddie Brown was a first-round draft pick from the University of Miami.

Tight end Rodney Holman made a Pro Bowl appearance with eight fellow Bengals.

coaching job with the Green Bay Packers. The new coach was Sam Wyche, who had been the quarterback coach for the San Francisco 49ers when they beat the Bengals in the Super Bowl.

ESIASON BECOMES A BOOMING SUCCESS

Wyche had been a quarterback with the Bengals when the team first began. As a coach with San Francisco, he helped develop the skills of Joe Montana. As a rookie head coach, Wyche would have a chance to work with a rookie quarterback, Boomer Esiason, who was picked by the Bengals in the second round of the 1984 draft.

Esiason came to the Bengals from the University of Maryland. He had a lot of ability and the confidence to match. His real name was Norman, but he was called Boomer because of the way he kicked in his mother's womb. Boomer had always been a star, but he would struggle in his first few years of pro football.

Anderson, who was in his mid-thirties, kept Esiason on the bench for a while, but soon Wyche was ready to use his quarterback of the future. Esiason replaced the aging Anderson, and the Bengals began to improve. In 1986, Esiason led Cincinnati to a 10-6 record. But 1987 was a different story.

Early in the season, the NFL Players Association decided to go on strike. The NFL owners decided they were going to play games anyway, using what they called "replacement" players. For Esiason, things were particularly difficult. He was the team's union representative, and he supported the strike. Unfortunately, the fans didn't. When the "real" players returned, the fans booed them, especially Esiason. "He was the target of all the hostility that built up among fans during the

Anthony Munoz was one of the greatest offensive tackles ever.

Safety David Fulcher was named to the Pro Bowl in recognition of his coverage skills.

strike," explained Mike Brown, Cincinnati's assistant general manager. "I don't think I've ever seen one player take the full force of a fan reaction that bad."

The fans may have booed Esiason, but Wyche never stopped believing in his quarterback, even though the Bengals finished 4-11 in 1987. "He's as competitive as any player in the game," Wyche said. "The great thing about Boomer is the way he can sense pressure and slide in the pocket to buy time until his receivers get open. It's a knack."

Esiason and Wyche were both under pressure to produce a winner. The fans wanted owner Paul Brown to fire Wyche after the 1987 season, but Brown wouldn't hear of it. Despite the vote of confidence, Wyche knew the Bengals had to be successful in 1988.

WOODS SHUFFLES INTO CINCINNATI

When the 1988 training camp began, a rookie fullback caught the eyes of the coaches. Elbert Woods—he preferred to be called "Ickey," a childhood nickname—an hard, and he ran over some people. During one of the practices, veteran offensive lineman Max Montoya walked up to Woods and said, "If you run the ball like that, you're going to make a lot of money in this league."

"After I said that," Montoya joked, "Ickey's eyes got real big." Woods had dreamed of being an NFL star since childhood. But Woods grew up in a bad neighborhood in Fresno, California—a neighborhood where kids often turn to crime and drugs. "Every night," Woods remembered, "you'd hear ambulances, police sirens and gunshots." And every night, his mother, Sylvia, would say to him, "You can do better that this."

Max Montoya (#65) played offensive guard with a fierce passion.

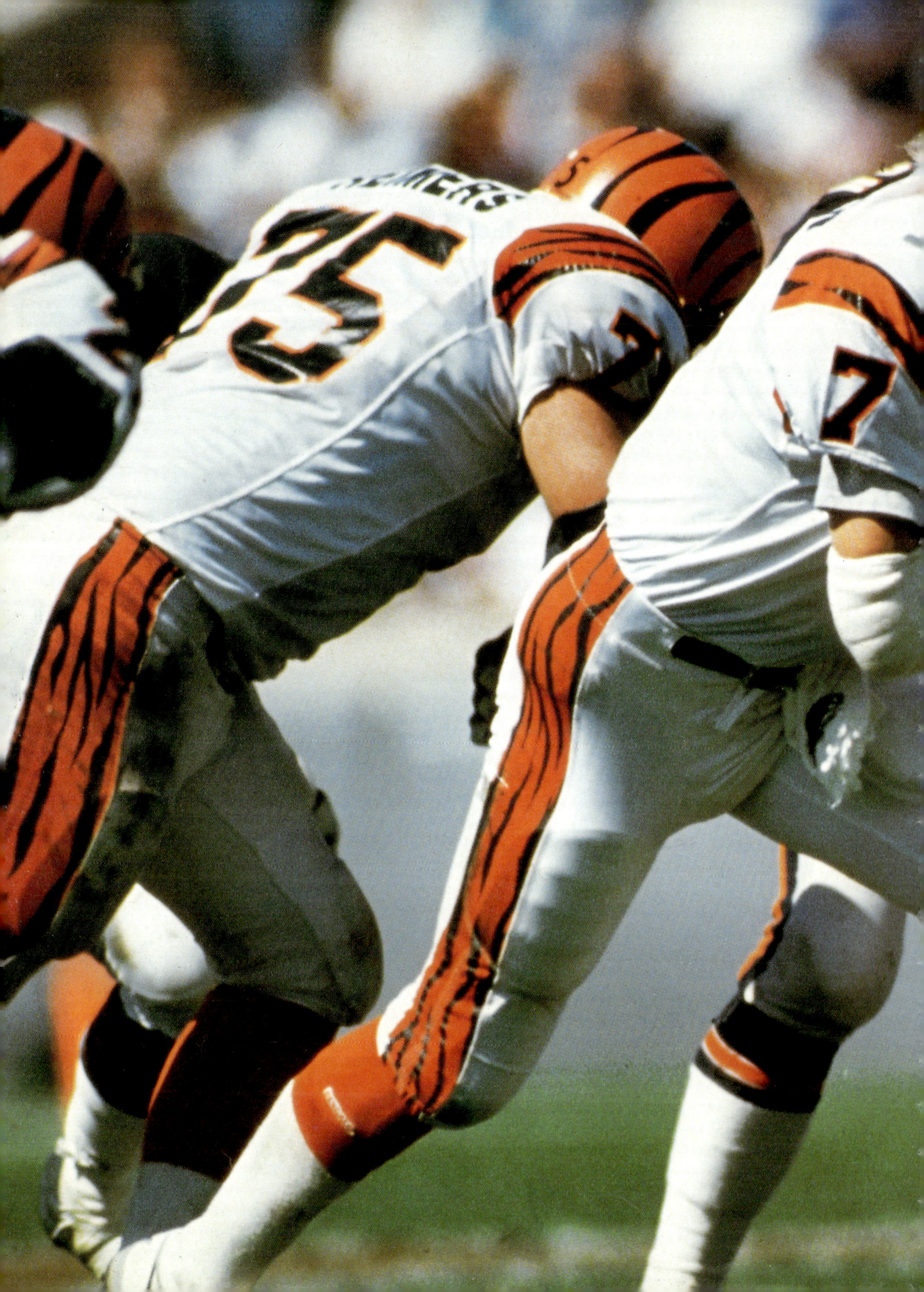

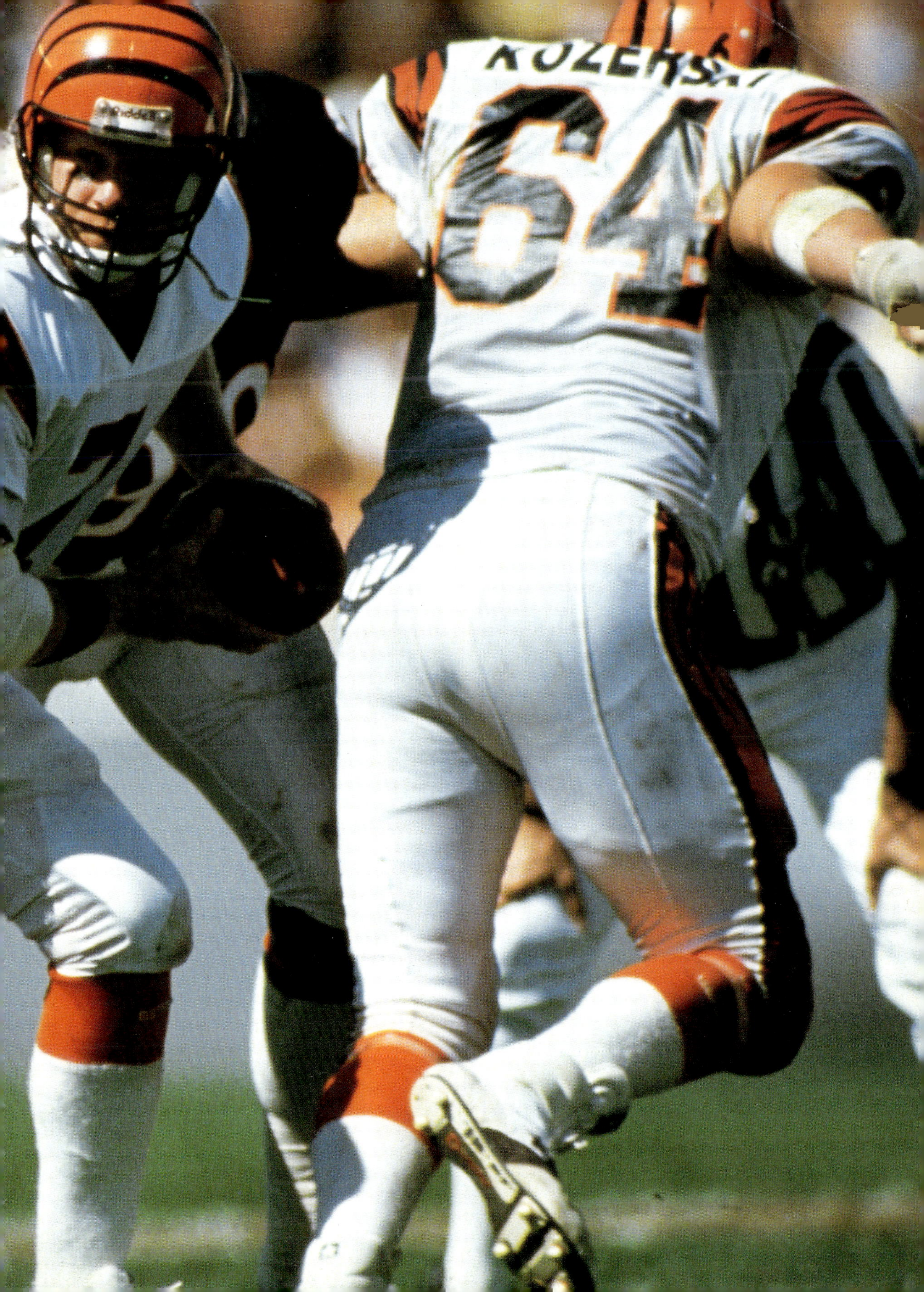
64

1989

Cornerback Eric Thomas made the Pro Bowl.

His football ability earned him a scholarship at the University of Nevada-Las Vegas. At UNLV, Woods and teammate Andre Horn, who was also from Fresno, talked constantly about making it in pro football. Horn would say to Woods, "You know you can make it. I know you can make it. Just hang in there, man. It'll happen."

Woods didn't become a star at UNLV until his senior year. When he finally got his opportunity on the field, Woods showed just how good he was. Off the field, however, Woods had to once more face the bitter realities of his impoverished background. His friend Horn had been shot and killed back home in Fresno. This tragedy only intensified Woods' determination to make it in the NFL.

At training camp with the Bengals, Woods showed such talent that Wyche soon put him in the starting line-up. Led by

Woods and Esiason, who was having the best year of any quarterback in the league, the Bengals raced to first place in the AFC Central Division and stayed there. The team was also entertaining to watch—especially Woods, who discovered a new way to celebrate touchdowns.

One night before a game, Woods was out with his mother. Ickey suddenly started to do a strange dance. He hopped a couple of times on one foot and then hopped a couple of times on the other foot. He finished by shaking his hips.

"What are you doing?" his mother asked.

"When I score tomorrow, I'm going to do this dance in the end zone," Ickey said.

"Boy," said his mother, "you better not."

But Woods did. He danced after every touchdown he scored. The Cincinnati media started calling it the "Ickey Shuffle." Soon, it seemed everybody was doing the Shuffle. Teammates were doing it. Fans were doing it. Even owner Paul Brown, who was eighty years old, did it once.

Woods gained more than 1,000 yards for the Bengals and scored 18 touchdowns during the 1988 season. As good as Woods was, Esiason was better and was named NFL Offensive Player of the Year. The Bengals defense was having a great year as well. Reggie Williams, one of the oldest linebackers in the league at age 34, was having one of his best seasons. Nose tackle Tim Krumrie was everywhere, leading the team in tackles.

The Bengals went 12-4 and won the AFC Central Division title. Cincinnati then beat Seattle and Buffalo to advance to the Super Bowl. The opponent was San Francisco, the same team that defeated the Bengals in the 1982 Super Bowl.

Cincinnati started slowly in the Super Bowl. The offense could

As a rookie, running back Harold Green rushed for an impressive 4.3 yards per carry average.

Wide receiver Cris Collinsworth.

not move, and the defense was having trouble holding down 49ers quarterback Joe Montana. Tragically for the Bengals, they lost Krumrie in the first period after he suffered a broken leg. The soul of the defense was gone, but the team didn't lose hope. Despite Montana's heroics, San Francisco could manage only a field goal in the first half, as the teams were tied 3-3 going into the locker room.

In the second half, Esiason found the range and Cincinnati took the lead 13-6 on a kickoff return for a touchdown by Stanford Jennings. But Montana hit Jerry Rice for the tying touchdown. Cincinnati got a field goal from Jim Breech, his third of the game. But then Montana broke the Bengals' hearts with a brilliant late-game drive for the winning touchdown with 34 seconds left. "Thirty-four seconds," Wyche muttered on the sidelines. "We were 34 seconds away." San Francisco won 20-16. The Bengals went home disappointed, but they still believed they had the ability to become NFL champs.

Unfortunately, injuries plagued Cincinnati during the 1989 season: Ickey Woods missed almost the whole year after tearing up his knee in the second game of the regular season. Esiason's sore shoulder bothered him most of the season. And although Krumrie made an amazing recovery from his broken leg, he wasn't the dominant player he had been in 1988. Despite the injuries, the Bengals finished 8-8 in 1989 and almost made the playoffs.

The team did make the playoffs in 1990, finishing the regular season with a 9-7 record and the AFC Central Division title. Running back James Brooks, who had stepped in for the injured Ickey Woods, continued his fine play by rushing for over 1,000 yards for the second consecutive season, while Esiason led a potent passing attack featuring wide receiver Eddie Brown. In the first-round Wild Card game, the Bengals battered the Houston

Wide receiver Eddie Brown caught 10 passes in a single game against the Chargers.

Left to right: Tim Krumrie, Ickey Woods, David Fulcher, Rickey Dixon.

Oilers 41-14. They lost to the Los Angeles Raiders 20-10 in the second round, but hopes were still high for the Bengals to dominate in the 1990s.

But then everything went wrong for Cincinnati, including an eight-game losing streak the following season. Injuries and declining performances by team veterans took their toll. The Cincinnati fans and media began to lambast both Esiason and Wyche. Bengals management was convinced that the team needed a new direction—both at head coach and at quarterback.

Dave Shula carried on the family tradition when he became head coach of the Bengals.

YOUNG SHULA TAKES CHARGE

To replace Sam Wyche, the Bengals named Dave Shula as their new head coach for the 1992 season. Shula was 32 and easily the youngest head coach in the NFL. But his background could not have prepared him better. His father, Don Shula, head coach of the Miami Dolphins, was the winningest NFL coach of all time. "I grew up around the game," Dave Shula said. "I was always interested in what I was doing around the game. I paid attention." Shula worked as an assistant coach under his father for seven years, then served as offensive coordinator for the Dallas Cowboys before taking the Bengals job.

Shula's first priority was to find a replacement for the aging Esiason. He made University of Houston quarterback David Klingler his number one pick in the 1992 NFL Draft, and by the end of the season Klingler had taken over as the team's starter. But the Bengals finished a disappointing 5-11. The final game of the season marked the end of the remarkable 13-year career of Bengals offensive tackle Anthony Munoz, whom most experts consider the finest at his position in NFL history. When

Tackles Bruce Remiers (#75) and Anthony Munoz (#78).

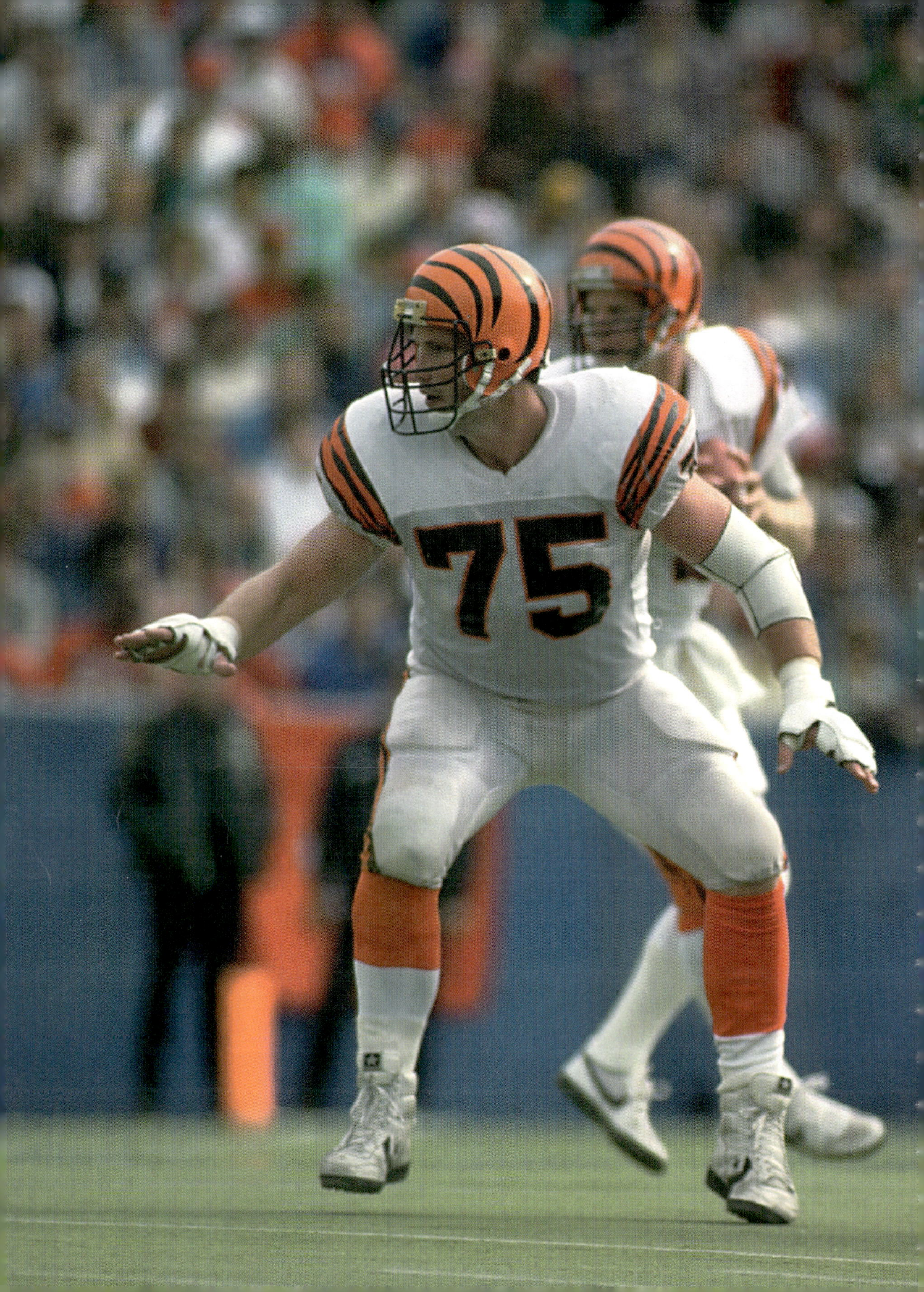

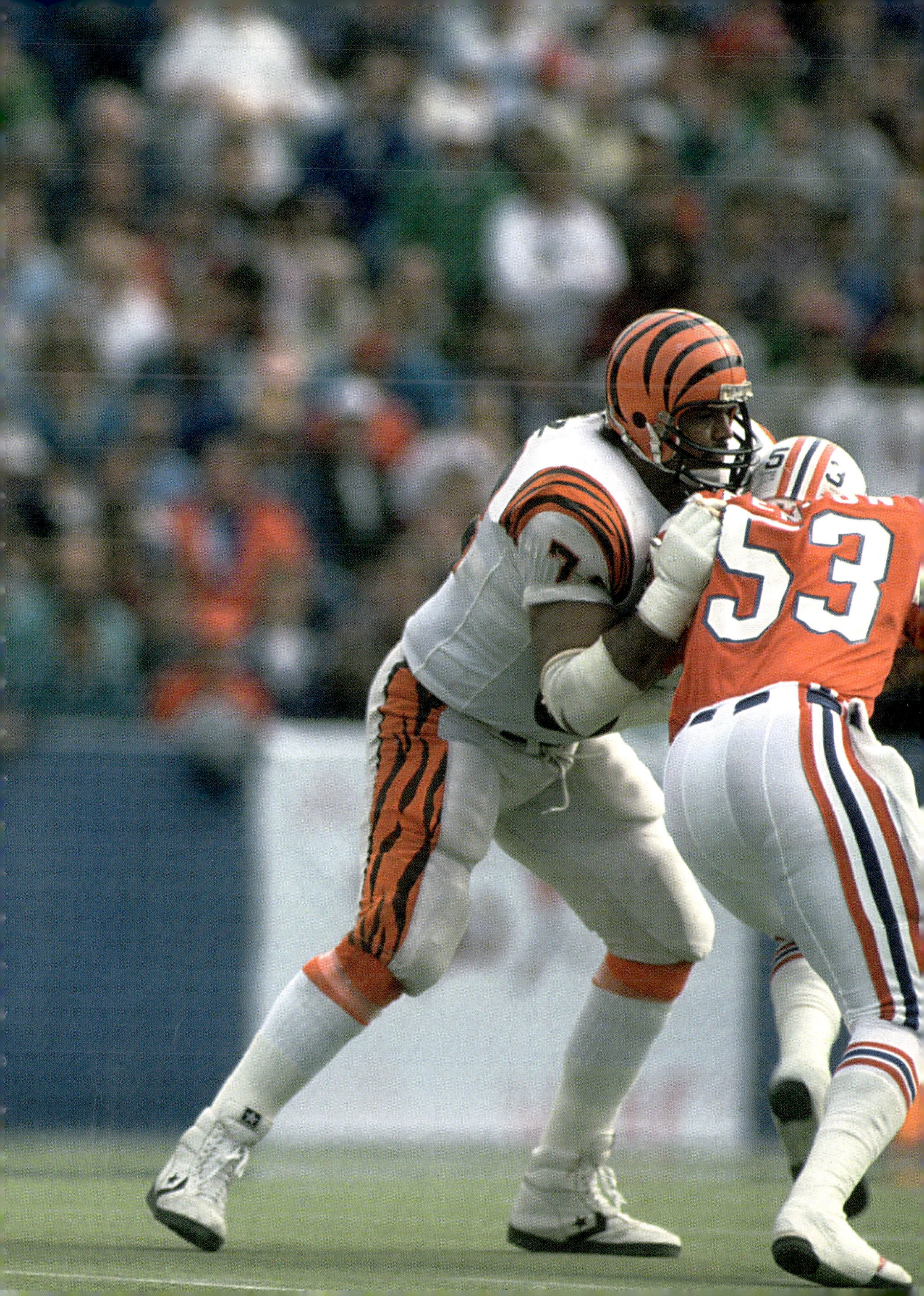
53

Cornerback Ashley Ambrose is one of the anchors of the Bengals' stingy pass defense.

Munoz was named to the Pro Bowl in 1992, it marked the 11th straight time that he had been so honored—more than any other NFL player.

The Bengals suffered through consecutive 3-13 records the next two seasons. The fans were restless and many called for the firing of Shula. But general manager Mike Brown stood by his coach. "Dave has done a good job under trying circumstances. Sometimes you can judge a person better when things don't go well than when they do go well. During these tough times, Dave has never wavered."

Things started to go much better in the second half of 1994, thanks to an unexpected change at the quarterback position. Klingler went down with an injury and back-up quarterback Jeff Blake took over. Blake, a former sixth-round draft pick by the New York Jets who had been waived by the club before catching on with the Bengals, set the league on fire with his unexpected offensive heroics. He threw four touchdown passes against the Houston Oilers and was named AFC Offensive Player of the Month for November, sparking what the Cincinnati media called "Blake-mania" amongst Bengals fans. Klingler recovered from his injuries, but Blake kept his starting job.

Bengals offensive coordinator Bruce Coslet praised his new leader. "Jeff showed himself to be a very good leader, a player guys will rally around. He has a strong arm, and was a very accurate deep passer. He needs to develop more consistency overall, but that's something that, for any quarterback, comes only with more practice and playing time."

In 1995, Blake did more than develop consistency—he became one of the stars of the league. He led all AFC quarterbacks with 28 touchdown passes, guided the Bengals to an improved 7-9 record and was named to the Pro Bowl along with his chief

Elusive running back Ki-Jana Carter joined the Bengals in 1995.

Jeff Blake emerged as an All-Pro quarterback in the 1990s.

Carl Pickens resists a Cardinal's tackle.

passing target, wide receiver Carl Pickens. Pickens gave Blake a deep threat, and he was also an exceptional leaper. Nor did he lack for confidence. "If the ball is up there high," Pickens said, "and I can get my feet planted, nine times out of ten I think I can go up and get it."

With its newfound, high-powered offense, the Bengals seem ready to claw their way back into title contention. After two close losses in the 1980s, a third trip to the Super Bowl would be a challenge the team would relish. For Cincinnati fans, the 1990s may yet be a time to roar.